Dedication

In loving memory of

Leonard O. Ayonote
&
Christopher O. Odia-Ogedegbe

Acknowledgements

I am sincerely grateful to all who have made these reflections of mine not just words in my heart but a reality for all to handle, feel, read and work with.

I especially acknowledge those whose materials are sources of my inspiration and those who contributed their quota in proofreading, criticising and making valuable suggestions. Worthy of mention is His Lordship, Most Rev. Dr. Gabriel G. Dunia, my Bishop and Father, for granting the Imprimatur, Rev. Fr. Prof. Anselm Jimoh for his brotherly encouragement, and for accepting to give the Nihil Obstat. To my bosom brother in the priesthood, Rev. Fr. Dr. Stan-William Ede, I thank you for the beautiful foreword and for suggesting the title of this book. May God, in his infinite goodness, reward your generosity.

To you who will pick up this book to read, I acknowledge you for your time spent on it; as you read through, let it guide and guard you in your life endeavours.

Lastly, I acknowledge all who have been a source of inspiration to me in my priestly ministry. May God bless and reward you all. Amen.

RHYMES FROM THE CLOUDS

Tips for Happier Living

Leonard O. ANETEKHAI

Rhymes from the Clouds: Tips for Happier Living

First Publication 2011
Allen Publishers, Benin City, Nigeria.

Production and publishing: BoD - Books on Demand, Norderstedt
ISBN: 9783757829032

Nihil Obstat: Rev. Fr. Prof. Anselm Jimoh
Department of Philosophy
Ss. Peter and Paul Seminary
Bodija, Ibadan.

Imprimatur: Most Rev. (Dr) Gabriel G. Dunia
Bishop, Catholic Diocese of Auchi

The Nihil Obstat and Imprimatur are official declarations that a book or pamphlet is free of doctrinal or moral error. There is no implication that those who have granted the Nihil Obstat and imprimatur agree with the contents, opinions or statements expressed.

Contents

Foreword

Human history is fraught with efforts, theories, and further efforts, all aimed at the achievement of harmonious coexistence and cooperation in human relationships, and in the sharing of goods, within local communities, national societies and on the international level. It is part of the social nature of human beings that we live in groups. And this requires that we have laws or rules that govern our relationships and interactions. Morality and religiously and culturally shared values are positive tools for social living, and for these to be effectuated, there must be at least some awareness of the social principles that tend towards the "good". Following from this knowledge, each individual begets the onus to situate himself within the context of an integrated life in society.

Unfortunately, however, we are living in an era of extraordinary socio-political, economic and cultural change. These changes are marked by the creation of great divisions and deep conflicts among people in society. There tends to be a neo-dimensional renewal of *"homo homini lupus"* (man's inhumanity to man), so that injustices, violence and disregard for human rights abound the world over. Terrorism has cast a dark shadow of despair, and the world itself has become a daily theatre of war amidst the incessant peace-talks, peace processes and peace road-maps. Most recently, the future of the human race is threatened by nuclear destruction as the arms race continues to escalate. We cannot refrain from mentioning that there are countless number of children suffering from malnutrition and diseases of various kinds, as well as people weighed down under the vestiges of political subjugation and socio-economic deprivations.

It is quite a surprising irony of history and facts that today's world, which is strikingly remarkable for an intense development of interpersonal interactions due to contemporary advancements in science and technology, is also afflicted by this kind of intense crisis of identity and belongingness between human beings. It is one of the essential properties of the human person that he can achieve true and full humanity by virtue of his nature and by means of belonging to a community of other human persons with whom he interacts. In modern times however, the fraternal tower has fallen, and individualism has led to a breakdown of true communion among human beings, the effect of which is a high-level disregard for the sanctity of personhood and interpersonal values.

In the beginning, God created the Heavens and the earth and all that they contain (cf. Gen 1:1-2:4). Then "God created man in his own image and likeness" (cf. Gen 1:27) and gave him a special dignity, crowned with glory and honour and given dominion over all other creatures (Ps 8:6-10). This, in fact, is a gratifying exaltation, a *special dignity* that applies to every man irrespective of age, tribe, gender, nationality or race, and is meant to be sacrosanctly respected and upheld by all. The Fathers of the Second Vatican Council put this succinctly in the following words: "All men are endowed with a rational soul and are created in God's image; they have the same nature and origin, and being redeemed by Christ, they enjoy the same divine call and destiny; there is here a *basic equality between all men,* and it must be given ever greater recognition" (cf. Vatican II, *Gaudium et Spes – Pastoral Constitution on the Church in the Modern World, 29*).

By an unfortunate twist of fate, man who was created wealthy in all ramifications has, by his own folly, distorted this exalted stance, for he danced astray, off the stage of glory upon which God has set him. What followed thereafter is a history of toils and successes, pains and joys, and sadly enough, the perpetuation of class differences and class struggles.

Well, the urgency resounds anew of the need to build a more human world through the furthering of truth, honesty, justice and peace. It's an indubitable fact that "all men are endowed with a rational soul and are created in God's image; they have the same nature and origin and, being redeemed by Christ, they enjoy the same divine calling and destiny; thus, there exists a basic equality between all men, and it must be given greater recognition" (Vatican II Council, *Gaudium et Spes*, 29). This constitutes the secret of sustaining the world on the pillars of peace and harmony.

Building a more human world in which the rights and dignity of every man are cherished and respected and in which fraternal love, social and international peace abound, have been the wish and exhortations of our Popes and Church leaders in history, especially in recent times. Hence many Encyclicals and Apostolic Letters have been issued along these lines. Reading the signs of the times, it is obvious that the issue of family life in the world through fraternisation should be evermore upheld with the hope that someday, all people would come to cherish these norms of human coexistence and progress.

On the other hand, building a more human world is a task that has to take root in each individual – from person to person, from whence it can then spread through groups of people, communities, and then to the world. Most of us know what is good, at least in principle. The difficulties arise in living out what we know and in the application of ideal religious values and moral knowledge to particular contexts. This book, **RHYMES FROM THE CLOUDS: TIPS FOR HAPPIER LIVING,** is a compendium of life and relational resource that addresses itself to each individual in a unique way, urging each one to heal the world and promote interpersonal interactions through a process that begins from the individual himself.

The author of the book, Rev. Fr. Leonard Anetekhai, a Catholic Priest, writes from a great depth of prayerful reflection, rapt conviction and personal experience. He is one who knows what it means to be happy and fulfilled and to make others happy in life. As a priest, he has ministered to people of all classes and various groupings; he has felt their respective joys, failures, hopes and aspirations and has firmly understood what makes the difference in each case; he has counselled many people facing different kinds of problems, and the desired result had been evident in those who complied with his counsel. In all of these, Fr. Anetekhai came to the realisation that most of the problems we face in society and the world arise from a personal crisis in the individual and the breakdown of inter-personal relations among groups of people, in society and, by extension, the world over.

In short but poetic and rhetorical chapters, Fr. Anetekhai has chosen to use a very simple but penetrative style to communicate his message to the world. He draws much from the wisdom of the wisest sages who have ever tread the face of the earth and makes extensive use of the Bible, making the book very much scriptural. The ingenuity of the book also comes from the author's ability to bring together a wide range of sapiential thought and a large collection of personality-development tips from variegated sources, simplify them and present them in very rewarding briefs – easy to read, inspiring to grasp, and desirable to practice.

I hereby recommend this book as a daily companion for everyone who desires to live a happier and more fulfilled life and who desires to make a positive impact on our world by healing the world and ridding it of all negative tendencies through the fostering of peace, justice, equality and love, all of which proceed from a balanced level of personal, inter-personal, intranational and international relations. And as Fr. Leo rightly implies from the tune of his sources and methodology, all of the above efforts to heal and build oneself, the society and the world can be fully achieved if we put God at the centre of our quest. Hence we always have to "look up to Jesus, the author and perfecter of our faith" (cf. Heb. 12:2).

REV. FR. DR. STAN-WILLIAM EDE
Rector, St. Thomas Aquinas Catholic Church, Ivioghe;
Vice-Rector, Immaculate Conception Seminary, Ivhianokpodi;

December 8, 2010,
Solemnity of the Immaculate Conception.

(Forward to the first edition)

Introduction

Rhymes from the Clouds: Tips for Happier Living is a book that deals with the realities of life. It draws inspiration from personal reflections on spiritual books and the words of the Preacher, Ben Sirach (Ecclesiasticus). This reflection focuses not just on personal transformation, but also on creating change in society. It is a common misconception to perceive the person next door as an enemy. However, it is often said that "Man is his own best friend and his worst enemy".

From the moment we are born, we cannot live isolated. We need others to survive. Despite the challenges that come with being human, we move from the beginning of life to its end. Therefore, we must acknowledge that genuine transformation begins with ourselves, no matter what we do.

I hope my little effort will help those who come across it to reckon with the facts of life, which must occur because we are relational beings. We must make that personal commitment, even when all odds are against us, to lead a holy life and bring others close to God.

We should, therefore, firmly note what George Carlin says: "Our life is not measured by the number of breaths we take, but by the moments that take our breath away".

Happy reading!

1

Life Is Relational (1)

As a people, we are part of a human family. Whether a woman lives in a mansion or a convent, whether she is a wife or a mistress – she is obligated to and dependent on someone else – at least one other person and usually more. Whether a man is a corporate executive or a pastor, the President of a country or a local community leader, he must relate to others.

Living apart from some kind of human relationship with certain reciprocal responsibilities is impossible. We do not – and we cannot live in isolation from one another. We depend on each other to achieve our individual and shared needs – physically, emotionally, socially and most importantly, spiritually.

Serving One Another:
Gene A. Getz.

Life Is Relational (II)

Do not exchange a friend for money or a real brother for the gold of Ophir. Do not dismiss a wise and good wife, for her charm is worth more than gold. Do not abuse slaves who work faithfully or hired labourers who devote themselves to their task. Let your soul love intelligent slaves; do not withhold from them their freedom.

Do you have cattle? Look after them; if they are profitable to you, keep them.
Do you have children? Discipline them and make them obedient from their youth.
Do you have daughters? Be concerned for their chastity, and do not show yourself too indulgent with them. Give a daughter in marriage, and you complete a great task, but give her to a sensible man.

Do you have a wife who pleases you? Do not divorce but uphold and cherish her to get the best from her. With all your heart, honour your father, and do not forget the birth pangs of your mother. Remember that you were born of your parents; how can you repay what they have given to you?

With all your soul, fear the Lord and revere his priests. With all your might, love your Maker, and do not neglect his ministers. Fear the Lord and honour the priest, and give him his portion, as you have been commanded: the first fruits, the guilt offering, the gift of the shoulders, the sacrifice of sanctification, and the first fruits of the holy things.

Stretch your hand to the poor, so your blessing may be complete. Give graciously to all the living; do not withhold kindness even from the dead. Do not avoid those who weep but mourn with those who mourn. Do not hesitate to visit the sick; you will be loved for such deeds. In all you do, remember the end of your life, and then you will never sin.

Ecclesiasticus 7: 18 – 36 NRSV.

Sacredness Of Life

Who can count the number of babies unborn because they have been killed in their mother's wombs, children abandoned and abused by their parents and children who grow up without affection and education?

In some countries, entire populations are deprived of housing and work, lacking the means absolutely essential for leading a life worthy of human dignity. They are deprived even of those things necessary for their sustenance. Significant areas of poverty and misery, both physical and moral, exist at this moment on the periphery of human dwelling. Entire groups of human beings have been seriously afflicted.

But the sacredness of the human person cannot be obliterated, no matter how often it is devalued and violated, because it has its unshakable foundation in God as Creator and Father.

Pope John Paul II.

4

When Life Is Unfair

Life is full of injustices. If we look, they are all around us: A mother loses her only child. An infertile couple with empty arms read in the dailies; of parents abusing (even murdering) their children. A beautiful teenage girl is paralysed in a car accident and then, shortly after, loses her mother to cancer — a widow with two children losing them to a fatal car accident on their way back from school.

Why? We may ask. Does this make any sense? Is human suffering ever going to end? We may consider these happenings as cause and effect or actions equal consequences. We teach and believe that what we sow, we reap. And for much of life, that is true. Yet there are those times when the unexplainable and unthinkable happens.

We recall the story of Job, a righteous man who suffered the loss of his children, possessions, and health. God withdrew His protection from him, and Satan was permitted to inflict harm as he tried to prove that Job was righteous only because God had incredibly blessed him. Not left to die, God restored his losses.

When a major loss happens, we often recoil with the whys. God can handle our questions while He patiently loves us through the process of our suffering. The good news to remember is that Jesus said, "In the world, you will have tribulations, but be of good cheer; I have overcome the world". (John 16:33)

Your New Life:
Walker L. Jeter.

5

Misery Of Human Life

Hard work was created for everyone,
and a heavy yoke is laid on the children
of Adam from the day they come forth from
their mother's womb until the day they
return to the mother of all the living.

Perplexities and fear of heart are theirs,
and anxious thoughts of the day of their death.
From the one who sits on a splendid throne
to the one who grovels in dust and ashes, from
the one who wears purple and a crown to the one
who is clothed in burlap, there is anger and envy
and trouble and unrest, and fear of death,
and fury and strife.

And when one rests upon his bed, his sleep
at night confuses his mind. He gets little or no rest;
he struggles in his sleep as he did by day.
He is troubled by the visions in his mind, like
one who has escaped from the battlefield.

At the moment he reaches safety, he wakes up,
astonished that his fears are groundless. To all
creatures, human and animal, but to sinners seven
times more, come death and bloodshed and strife and
sword, calamities and famine and ruin and plague.

All these were created for the wicked, and on their account, the flood came. All that is of earth returns to earth, and what is from above returns above.

Ecclesiasticus 40: 1 – 11 NRSV.

The Joys Of Life

Wealth and wages make life sweet,
but better than either is finding a treasure.
Children and the building of a city establish
one's name, but better than either is the one
who finds wisdom. Cattle and orchards make
one prosperous, but a blameless wife is better
than either.

Wine and music gladden the heart, but the
love of friends is better than either. The flute
and the harp make a sweet melody, but a pleasant
voice is better than either. The eye desires grace
and beauty, but the green shoots of grain more
than either.

A friend or companion is always welcome,
but a sensible wife is better than either. Kindred
and helpers are for a time of trouble, but
almsgiving rescues better than either. Gold and
silver make one stand firm, but good counsel is
esteemed more than either.

Riches and strength build up confidence,
but the fear of the Lord is better than either.
There is no want in the fear of the Lord, and
with it, there is no need to seek for help.

The fear of the Lord is like a garden of blessings
and covers a person better than any glory.

Ecclesiasticus 40: 18 – 27 NRSV.

7

All Have Sinned

"There is none righteous, no, not one;
There is none who understands; There is none
who seeks after God. They have all turned aside;
they have together become unprofitable;
there is none who does good, no, not one.
Their throat is an open tomb; with their tongues,
they have practised deceit.

The poison of asps is under their lips, their mouth
full of cursing and bitterness. Their feet are swift to
shed blood; destruction and misery are in their ways.

And the way of peace they have not known.
There is no fear of God before their eyes. Now we
know that whatever the law says, it says to those
under the law, that every mouth may be stopped,
and all the world may become guilty before God.

Therefore, by the deeds of the law, no flesh
will be justified in His sight, for by the law
is the knowledge of sin.

Romans 3: 9 – 20.

8

What Happens If We Sin?

When we accept Jesus Christ into our life,
we become sons and daughters of God. We have
begun a new life. We have been born again.
Just as we were born into a human family, so, by
trusting in Jesus, we are born into God's family:
It is written: "As many as received him, he gave
them the power to become the children of God."
(John 1: 12).

He thus becomes our Father; we become His children.
There is a relationship between us which can never be
undone. This does not mean we become perfect
overnight. We still sin, however hard we try not to.

Well then, what happens if we sin?
A little boy playing in his father's garden destroyed
some of the crops in it, and he had been cautioned not
to play there. At mealtime, there was dead silence, for
he had disobeyed his father. This lasted until he
owned up and said, Daddy, I am sorry.

The relationship remained unchanged;
he is still a son. His father could disown him, but he
never ceases to be his son. It was the friendship that
was broken until the little boy was able to say,
"I am sorry".

When we disobey Christ or are inconsiderate or lazy, when we do, say, or think something we know to be wrong, we are still children of God; the relationship has not changed, and all we must do is ask for mercy. We have spoiled our friendship with him, and it is up to us to say, "Lord, I am sorry".

9

Self – Control

Do not follow your base desires but restrain your appetites. Allowing your soul to take pleasure in base, desire will make you the laughingstock of your enemies. Do not revel in great luxury, or you may become impoverished by its expense. Do not become a beggar by feasting on borrowed money when you have nothing in your purse. The one who does this will not become rich; one who despises small things will fail little by little. Wine and women lead intelligent men astray, and the man who consorts with prostitutes is reckless. Decay and worms will take possession of him, and the reckless person will be snatched away.

One who trusts others too quickly has a shallow mind and one who sins does wrong to himself. One who rejoices in wickedness will be condemned, but one who hates gossip has less evil. Never repeat a conversation, and you will lose nothing at all. With friend or foe, do not report it, and unless it would be a sin for you, do not reveal it; for someone may have heard you and watched you and in time will hate you. Have you heard anything? Let it die with you. Be brave; it will not make you burst! Having heard something, the fool suffers birth pangs like a woman in labour with a child. Like an arrow stuck in a person's thigh, so is gossip inside a fool.

Question a friend; perhaps he did not do it, or if he did, so that he may not do it again. Question a neighbour; perhaps he did not say it, or if he said it, so that he may not repeat it. Question a friend, for often it is slander; so, do not believe everything you hear. A person may make a slip without intending it. Who has not sinned with his tongue? Question your neighbour before you threaten him, and let the law of the Most High take its course.

Ecclesiasticus 18: 30 – 32; 19: 1 - 19 NRSV.

10

Inner Beauty

In our age and time, everybody wants to look good.
This is important, people say, to have the right image.
It enhances our ministry, business, and personal
and corporate self-esteem.

Looking good is an enormous task. Millions of money
is spent on cosmetics, face-lifts (Surgery), hair
treatments, nail treatment and any other beauty
treatment possible.

One cannot help but compare this to how much time is
spent on developing the intellect and character traits
that last. While it is true that we should do the best we
can with what we have physically, we must remember
that our outward beauty will fade, and we will all look
old. Then, what will be of our inner beauty when
death comes knocking?

Your New Life:
Walker L. Jeter.

11

Nothing Is New

The wind goes towards the south and turns around to the north; the wind whirls about continually and comes again on its circuit. All the rivers run into the sea, yet the sea is not full; to the place from which the rivers come, there they return. All things are full of labour; Man cannot express it. The eye is not satisfied with seeing, nor is the ear filled with hearing. That which has been is what will be, that which is done is what will be done, and there is nothing new under the sun.

Is there anything of which it may be said, 'See, this is new?' It has already been in ancient times before us. There is no remembrance of former things, nor will there be any remembrance of things that are to come by those who will come after.

I, the Preacher, was king over Israel in Jerusalem. And I set my heart to seek and search out by wisdom concerning all that is done under heaven; this burdensome task God has given to the sons of man, by which they may be exercised. I have seen all the works under the sun; indeed, all is vanity and grasping for the wind.

What is crooked cannot be made straight, and what is lacking cannot be numbered. I communed with my heart, saying, Look, I have attained greatness and gained more wisdom than all before me in Jerusalem. My heart has understood great wisdom and knowledge. And I set my heart to know wisdom and madness and folly. I perceived that this also is grasping for the wind. For in much wisdom is much grief, and he who increases knowledge increases sorrow.

Ecclesiasticus 19: 6 – 18 NRSV.

12

What about My Brother Next Door?

We live in a world of incredible human needs. Hundreds of people are poor and hungry, homeless and illiterate, battered by illness and die young. Some have the means and food to eat but cannot, while others languish in poverty and daily wants.

In some developing countries, people are prepared to risk their lives to travel on rickety boats adrift at sea or live in overcrowded refugee camps without facilities, searching for greener pastures.

In our time, we see the extermination of people in the so-called developing nations, both young and old, dying because the help that comes to them, if it comes at all, is too little and comes too late.

There are many other examples globally of people in great need of the most necessities. That we can feed means we have to feed ourselves, but does the contrast of having nothing to eat mean anything to us?

13

In Communion with Him

No matter where we turn, our world's difficulty and splendour tell us we have a Creator. If so, our lives belong to HIM; we do not exist for ourselves alone but to give Him glory and to be in a deep, personal relationship with him.

This relationship spurs us to greater consciousness of God's presence in our lives. Without the Lord being there, life seems haphazard and worthless. But when we are in communion with HIM, he brings order and peace to our lives. We begin to see that we are not an accident. We are part of a magnificent design far bigger than we can imagine.

Power to Produce

The wisest man who ever lived said, "My son, attend to my words; incline thine ear unto my sayings. Let them not depart from thine eyes, keep them in the midst of thine heart". (Proverbs 4: 20-21).

The seeds of happiness, success, health and prosperity are given to you by God. And He gave you the right to plant them. The poorest man on earth has as much right as anyone else to plant these seeds of success and prosperity and reap a harvest in his life.

Every seed has in it the miraculous power to reproduce itself manifold. But it must be planted. Once you do that, God has granted it the mysterious power to grow.

You can have plenty instead of doing without, have health instead of being sick, have peace instead of living under pressure, prosper instead of living in poverty, and be a winner instead of a loser.
All you need is to work hard.

How to Enjoy Plenty:
T. L. Osborn.

15

Not Alone

As a child of God, people at school, workplaces
and in the public sphere will watch to see if your
life reflects in your words. Be thorough and proficient
in your work and honest in all your dealing; keep calm
when your faith is attacked or laughed at; be ready
to speak out at injustices; and be prepared to show
what Christ means to you personally when the
opportunity comes.

Be an active Christian, one who can be trusted.
The most extraordinary job we have been created
for is winning others for Christ. This requires a
genuine love for Christ and real love for people.
It will mean praying for them, caring for them,
getting to know them, sharing their interest and
talking naturally about Christian life.

The way ahead will not be easy, but you are not alone
- Jesus Christ goes along with you all the way.

The Family

The family is the smallest unit of the Church and human world and merits special attention. The family is the cell of society, the domestic Church, and the birthplace of every child. The family is essential for the well-being of society and the Church. When the family is sick, society and the Church get infected.

As a people of God, we are to collectively and individually make efforts to protect the family from the world's diseases. The diseases of disrespect, irresponsibility, waywardness, stealing, contraception, abortion, divorce, hedonism, materialism, and the like are fast eroding the dignity of family life and family existence in our society.

As the first point of civilisation, the individual family promotes the goodness and focus of every family, which God wants us to be. Let us be brothers and sisters to each other so that when we meet a larger family than ours, we will spread our God-given talents.

17

Duties to Parents

Listen to me, your father, O children; act accordingly, that you may be kept in safety. For the Lord honours a father above his children, and he confirms a mother's right over her children. Those who honour their father atone for sins, and those who respect their mother are like those who lay up treasure. Those who honour their father will have joy in their own children, and when they pray, they will be heard. Those who respect their father will have a long life, and those who honour their mother obey the Lord; they will serve their parents as their masters.

Honour your father by word and deed that his blessing may come upon you. For a father's blessing strengthens the houses of the children, but a mother's curse uproots their foundations. Do not glorify yourself by dishonouring your father, for your father's dishonour is no glory to you. The glory of one's father is one's own glory, and it is a disgrace for children not to respect their mother.

My child, help your father in his old age, and do not grieve him as long as he lives; even if his mind fails, be patient with him; because you have all your faculties, do not despise him. For kindness to a father will not be forgotten and will be credited to you against your sins;

in the day of your distress, it will be remembered in your favour; like frost in fair weather, your sins will melt away. Whoever forsakes a father is like a blasphemer, and whoever angers a mother is cursed by the Lord

Ecclesiasticus 3: 1 – 16 NRSV.

Bringing up Children

He who loves his son will whip him often so that
he may rejoice at the way he turns out. He who
disciplines his son will profit from him and boast of
him among acquaintances. He who teaches his son
will make his enemies envious and will glory in him
among his friends.

When the father dies, he will not seem to be dead,
for he has left behind him one like himself, whom in
his life he looked upon with joy and at death, without
grief. He has left behind him an avenger against his
enemies and one to repay the kindness of his friends.

Whoever spoils his son will bind up his wounds
and suffer heartache at every cry. An unbroken horse
turns out stubborn, and an unchecked son turns out
headstrong. Pamper a child, and he will terrorise you;
play with him, and he will grieve you.

Do not laugh with him, or you will have sorrow
with him, and in the end, you will gnash your teeth.
Give him no freedom in his youth, and do not ignore
his errors. Bow down his neck in his youth and beat
his sides while he is young, or else he will become
stubborn and disobey you, and you will have sorrow
of soul from him. Discipline your son and make his

yoke heavy so you may not be offended by his shamelessness.

Ecclesiasticus 30: 1 – 13 NRSV.

19

Back to The Father

Breaking up the fallow ground not only
includes repentance, but it also includes
returning to the Father. Some of us once
knew Him; we walked with Him and were
faithful to Him. We had the glory of the Father
on our spirit and His guidance for our life.
But today, it is all memories. Is this my case?

Dear, be reminded that the Father still loves us
and longs for us to be His. He calls us to come
back to Him! The prodigal who went to a far
country and wasted everything with uncontrollable
living imagined that all was lost! Yet came that
inward pull to go back to the Father's house.

God puts that inward pull in us daily,
and He invites us to come back to Him!
You may be travelling at the moment, or in your
classroom, even in your office, any place of relaxation:
God is saying it is time to return to me,
your FATHER.

Discovering True Value

Traditional religion has given a limited concept of
God's relationship with those who believe in Him.
Walking with God is generally considered an
experience reserved for a few who have consecrated
themselves to a state of material poverty and physical
suffering. One will have to break his or her way out of
the misconception of God – and will only do it if one
wants God's blessing and prosperity.

There are two schools of human thought.
One argues that man's greatest need is relaxation,
ease, pleasure, and freedom from pressure – to simply
live, breathe, eat, and love. The other school argues
that man's most basic need is for meaning,
significance, and purpose in life.

Well, you can choose the attitude towards life that
appeal to you. But one thing is sure; if you ever hope
to accomplish anything for yourself, others and God,
you will need to discover the miracle – God at work in
man and God's wonderful purpose for you in this life.
Discover your true value, your dynamic potential for
happiness, health, success and prosperity with God.

How to Enjoy Plenty:
T. L. Osborn.

Faithfulness to God

My child, when you come to serve the Lord,
prepare yourself for testing. Set your heart right,
be steadfast, and do not be impetuous in times of
calamity. Cling to him and do not depart, so that
your last days may be prosperous. Accept whatever
befalls you, and in times of humiliation, be patient.
For gold is tested in the fire, and those found
acceptable, in the furnace of humiliation. Trust in him,
and he will help you; make your way straight
and hope in him.

You who fear the Lord, wait for his mercy; do not
stray, or else you may fall. You who fear the Lord,
trust in him, and your reward will not be lost.
You who fear the Lord, hope for good things, for
lasting joy and mercy. Consider the generations of old
and see: has anyone trusted in the Lord and been
disappointed? Or has anyone persevered in the fear of
the Lord and been forsaken? Or has anyone called
upon him and be neglected? For the Lord is
compassionate and merciful; he forgives sins and
saves in time of distress.

Woe to timid hearts and to slack hands and to the
sinner who walks a double path! Woe to the
fainthearted who have no trust! Therefore, they will

have no shelter. Woe to you who have lost your nerve! What will you do when the Lord's reckoning comes?

Those who fear the Lord do not disobey his words, and those who love him keep his ways. Those who fear the Lord seek to please him and those who love him are filled with his law. Those who fear the Lord prepare their hearts and humble themselves before him. Let us fall into the hands of the Lord, but not into the hands of mortals; for equal to his majesty is his mercy, and equal to his name are his works.

Ecclesiasticus 2: 1 – 18 NRSV.

22

A Face Of Sorrow

In contemplating Christ's face, we confront the most paradoxical aspect of his mystery, as it emerges in his last hour on the cross — the mystery within the mystery, before which we cannot but prostrate ourselves in adoration.

The intensity of the episode of agony in the Garden of Olives passes before our eyes. Oppressed by foreknowledge of the trials that await him and alone before the Father, Jesus cries out to him in his habitual and affectionate expression of trust: "Abba Father". He asks him to take away, if possible, the cup of suffering.

But the Father seems not to want to heed the son's cry. To bring man back to the Father's face, Jesus not only had to take on the face of man, but he had to burden himself with the face of sin. "For our sake he made him to be sin who knew no sin, so that in him we might become the righteousness of God". (2 Cor. 5:21)

Pope John Paul II.

23

Do Not Be Discouraged

Do not be discouraged if you have a hard time doing what is right. When a person is born again, he is truly a child of God but still has to learn how to walk. When a new Christian makes a mistake, the devil tries to discourage him by making him think: "Now look at what I have done. I must act differently".

Some new Christians become confused and give way to doubt. They think: "I cannot live a Christian life; it is too hard for me. I might as well go back to my old life and not try to serve God". Besides, I do not see the great change in myself that the Christians talk about. I do not feel any joy of salvation; I guess I am not a Christian at all.

Have you ever struggled with some of these doubts? Remember that they come from your enemy trying to discourage you and make you fall. Some people feel more joy than others when they get saved, so do not worry about how you feel. The more you learn about what God did when He made you His child, the more joy you will have. As you thank Him for His blessings, your joy will grow. Remember that your salvation does not depend on what you feel or do not feel; it depends on the faithfulness of God, to whom you have given your life and soul.

If you have stumbled and fallen, it does not mean that you cannot learn to walk or that you are not God's child. Ask His forgiveness for your failures and then get up and try again.

As to the change in yourself, your desire to please God and the fact that you worry over your failures are proofs of a new nature. So, do not be discouraged. Remember that some children have more trouble than others in learning to walk.

Your New Life:
Walker L. Jeter.

24

Humility

My child perform your tasks with humility; then you will be loved by those whom God accepts. The greater you are, the more you must humble yourself; so you will find favour in the sight of the Lord. For great is the might of the Lord; but by the humble he is glorified.

Neither seek what is too difficult for you, nor investigate what is beyond your power. Reflect upon what you have been commanded, for what is hidden is not your concern. Do not meddle in matters beyond you, for more than you can understand has been shown you. For their conceit has led many astray, and wrong opinion has impaired their judgment.

Without eyes, there is no light; without knowledge, there is no wisdom. A stubborn mind will fare badly at the end, and whoever loves danger will perish in it. A stubborn mind will be burdened by troubles, and the sinner adds sin to sins.

When calamity befalls the proud, there is no healing, for an evil plant has taken root in him. The mind of the intelligent appreciates proverbs, and an attentive ear is the desire of the wise.

Ecclesiasticus 3: 17 – 29 NRSV.

25

The Spirit Of Contentment

As humans, we are open to so many wants and needs of life. Most of the time, we do not know which to fall to our wants or needs because we lack the spirit of contentment.

Contentment speaks of security – knowing who we are, knowing our purpose in life and believing we are always living out that purpose in fear of God.

Sometimes we avoid settling for contentment because we fear apathy. We want to excel; we want the best – and that is good. The important thing is to check our focus. What are we striving to achieve in life? What is our purpose in living? How do we use things around us?

To be content or at peace with ourselves, we must be grateful to God by letting his peace rule our hearts. We must learn to trust God by faith, and we must have an appropriate attitude toward things. Church Swindoll once said, "If you love people, you will use things; if you love things, you will use people."

26

Almsgiving

As water extinguishes a blazing fire, so almsgiving atones for sin. Those who repay favours give thought to the future; when they fall, they will find support.

My child do not cheat the poor of their living and do not keep needy eyes waiting. Do not grieve the hungry or anger one in need. Do not add to the troubles of the desperate or delay giving to the needy. Do not reject a suppliant in distress or turn your face away from the poor. Do not avert your eye from the needy and give no one reason to curse you; for if in bitterness of soul, some should curse you, their Creator will hear their prayer.

Endear yourself to the congregation; bow your head low to the great. Give a hearing to the poor and return their greeting politely. Rescue the oppressed from the oppressor, and do not be hesitant in giving a verdict. Be a father to orphans and be like a husband to their mother; you will then be like a son of the Most High, and he will love you more than does your mother.

Ecclesiasticus 3: 30 – 31, 4: 10 NRSV.

27

Pride, Not A Blessing

Do not get angry with your neighbour for every
injury, and do not resort to acts of insolence.
Arrogance is hateful to the Lord and to mortals, and
injustice is outrageous to both. Sovereignty passes
from nation to nation on account of injustice and
insolence, and wealth.

How can dust and ashes be proud?
Even in life, the human body decays. A long illness
baffles the physician; the king of today will die
tomorrow. For when one is dead, he inherits
maggots and vermin and worms.

The beginning of human pride is to forsake the Lord;
the heart has withdrawn from its Maker. For the
beginning of pride is sin, and the one who clings to it
pours out abominations. Therefore, the Lord brings
upon them unheard-of calamities and destroys them
completely.

The Lord overthrows the thrones of rulers and
enthrones the lowly in their place. The Lord plucks up
the roots of the nations and plants the humble in their
place. The Lord lays waste the lands of the nations
and destroys them to the foundations of the earth.

He removes some of them, destroys them, and erases
their memory from the earth.
Pride was not created for human beings, or violent
anger for those born of women.

Ecclesiasticus 10: 6 – 18 NRSV.

Self – Confidence

Watch for the opportune time, beware of evil, and do not be ashamed to be yourself. There is a shame that leads to sin, and there is a shame that is glory and favour. Do not show partiality, to your own harm or deference, to your downfall. Do not refrain from speaking at the right moment, and do not hide your wisdom. For wisdom becomes known through speech and education through the words of the tongue.

Never speak against the truth but be ashamed of your ignorance. Do not be ashamed to confess your sins, and do not try to stop the current of a river. Do not subject yourself to a fool or show partiality to a ruler. Fight to the death for truth, and the Lord God will fight for you.

Do not be reckless in your speech or sluggish and remiss in your deeds. Do not be like a lion in your home or suspicious of your servants. Do not let your hand be stretched out to receive and closed when it is time to give.

Ecclesiasticus 4: 20 – 31 NRSV.

29

Self -Examination

Before you speak, learn, and before you fall ill, take care of your health. Before judgment comes, examine yourself; and at the time of scrutiny, you will find forgiveness. Before falling ill, humble yourself; and when you have sinned, repent.

Let nothing hinder you from paying a vow promptly, and do not wait until death to be released from it. Before making a vow, prepare yourself; do not be like one who puts the Lord to the test. Think of his wrath on the day of death and of the moment of vengeance when he turns away his face.

In the time of plenty, think of the time of hunger; in days of wealth, think of poverty and need. From morning to evening, conditions change; all things move swiftly before the Lord. One who is wise is cautious in everything; when sin is all around, one guards against wrongdoing.

Every intelligent person knows wisdom and praises the one who finds her. Those who are skilled in words become wise themselves and pour forth apt proverbs.

Ecclesiasticus 18: 19 – 29 NRSV.

30

Choice of Friends

Do not abandon old friends, for new ones cannot equal them. A new friend is like new wine; you can drink it with pleasure when it has aged.

Do not envy the success of sinners, for you do not know what their end will be like. Do not delight in what pleases the ungodly; remember that they will not be held guiltless all their lives.

Keep far from those who have the power to kill, and the fear of death will not haunt you. But if you approach them, make no misstep, or they may rob you of your life. Know that you are stepping among snares and walking on the city battlements.

As much as you can, aim to know your neighbours, and consult with the wise. Let your conversation be with intelligent people, and let all your discussion be about the law of the Most High. Let the righteous be your dinner companions, and let your glory be in the fear of the Lord.

Ecclesiasticus 9: 10 – 16 NRSV.

31

Be on Guard with Your Friends

Pleasant speech multiplies friends, and a gracious tongue multiplies courtesies. Let those friendly with you be many, but let your advisers be one in a thousand. When you gain friends, gain them through testing and do not trust them hastily.

Some friends are such when it suits them, but they will not stand by you in times of trouble. And some friends change into enemies and tell of the quarrel to your disgrace. And there are friends who sit at your table, but they will not stand by you in times of trouble.

When you are prosperous, they become your second self, and Lord, it over your servants; but if you are brought low, they turn against you and hide from you. Keep away from your enemies and be on guard with your friends.

Faithful friends are a sturdy shelter: whoever finds one has found a treasure. Faithful friends are beyond price; no amount can balance their worth. Faithful friends are life-saving medicine and those who fear the Lord will find them. Those who fear the Lord direct their friendship aright, for as they are, so are their neighbours.

Ecclesiasticus 6: 5 – 17 NRSV.

Be Careful of Those You Call Friends (1)

Do not invite everyone into your home, for many are the tricks of the crafty. Like a decoy partridge in a cage, so is the mind of the proud, and like spies, they observe your weakness; for they lie in wait, turning good into evil, and to worthy actions, they attach blame.

From a spark, many coals are kindled, and a sinner lies in wait to shed blood. Beware of scoundrels, for they devise evil, and they may ruin your reputation forever. Receive strangers into your home, and they will stir up trouble for you and will make you a stranger to your own family.

If you do good, know whom you do it, and you will be thanked for your good deeds. Do good to the devout, and you will be repaid — if not by them, certainly by the Most High. No good comes to one who persists in evil or to one who does not give alms. Give to the devout, but do not help the sinner.

Do good to the humble, but do not give to the ungodly; hold back their bread, and do not give it to them, for by means of it they might subdue you; then you will receive twice as much evil for all the good you have done to them. For the Most High also hates sinners and will inflict punishment on the ungodly. Give to the one who is good, but do not help the sinner.

A friend is not known in prosperity, nor is an enemy hidden in adversity. One's enemies are friendly when one prospers, but in adversity, even one's friend disappears. Never trust your enemy, for like corrosion in copper, so is his wickedness. Even if he humbles himself and walks bowed down, take care to be on your guard against him. Be to him like one who polishes a mirror, to be sure it does not become completely tarnished.

Do not put him next to you; he may overthrow you and take your place. Do not let him sit at your right hand, or else he may try to take your own seat, and at last, you will realise the truth of my words and be stung by what I have said.

Who pities a snake charmer when he is bitten, or all those who go near wild animals? So, no one pities a person who associates with a sinner and becomes involved in the other's sins. He stands by you for a while, but he will not be there if you falter.

An enemy speaks sweetly with his lips, but in his heart, he plans to throw you into a pit; an enemy may have tears in his eyes, but if he finds an opportunity, he will never have enough of your blood. If evil comes upon you, you will find him ahead of you; pretending to help, he will trip you up. Then he will shake his head, clap his hands, whisper, and show his true face.

Ecclesiasticus 11: 29 –; 12 NRSV.

Be Careful of Those You Call Friends (II)

Whoever touches pitch gets dirty, and whoever associates with a proud person becomes like him. Do not lift a weight too heavy for you or associate with one mightier and richer than you. How can the clay pot associate with the iron kettle? The pot will strike against it and be smashed.

A rich person does wrong, and even adds insults; a poor person suffers wrong and must add apologies. A rich person will exploit you if you can be of use to him, but he will abandon you if you are in need. If you own something, he will live with you and drain your resources without a qualm.

When he needs you, he will deceive you, smile at and encourage you; he will speak to you kindly and say, "What do you need?" He will embarrass you with his delicacies until he has drained you two or three times, and finally, he will laugh at you. Should he see you afterwards, he will pass you by and shake his head at you.

Take care not to be led astray and humiliated when you are enjoying yourself. When an influential person invites you, be reserved, and he will invite you more insistently. Do not be forward, or you may be rebuffed; do not stand aloof, or you will be forgotten. Do not try to treat him as an equal or trust his lengthy conversations; for he will test you by prolonged talk, and while he smiles, he will be examining you. Cruel are those who do not keep your secrets; they will not spare you harm or imprisonment. Be on your guard and incredibly careful, for you are walking about with your own downfall.

Every creature loves its like, and every person the neighbour. All living beings associate with their own kind, and people stick close to those like themselves. What does a wolf have in common with a lamb? No more has a sinner with the devout. What peace is there between a hyena and a dog? And what peace between the rich and the poor? Wild asses in the wilderness are the prey of lions; likewise, the poor are feeding grounds for the rich. Humility is an abomination to the proud; likewise, the poor are an abomination to the rich.

When the rich person totters, he is supported by friends, but when the humble falls, he is pushed away even by friends. If the rich person slips, many come to the rescue; he speaks unseemly words, but they justify him. If the humble person slips, they even criticise him; he talks sense but is not given a hearing. The rich person speaks, and all are silent; they extol to the clouds what he says. The poor person speaks, and they say, 'Who is this fellow?' And should he stumble, they even push him down.

Riches are good if they are free from sin; poverty is evil only in the opinion of the ungodly. The heart changes the countenance, either for good or for evil. The sign of a happy heart is a cheerful face, but to devise proverbs requires painful thinking. Happy are those who do not blunder with their lips and need not suffer remorse for sin. Happy are those whose hearts do not condemn them, and who have not given up their hope.

Ecclesiasticus 13 – 14: 1 – 2 NRSV.

Be Friends to your Friends

One who pricks the eye brings tears, and one who pricks the heart makes clear its feelings. One who throws a stone at birds scares them away, and one who reviles a friend destroys a friendship.

Even if you draw your sword against a friend, do not despair, for there is a way back. If you open your mouth against your friend, do not worry, for reconciliation is possible. But as for reviling, arrogance, disclosure of secrets, or a treacherous blow — in these cases any friend will take to flight.

Gain the trust of your neighbour in his poverty, so that you may rejoice with him in his prosperity. Stand by him in time of distress, so that you may share with him in his inheritance.
The vapour and smoke of the furnace precede the fire; so, insults precede bloodshed. I am not ashamed to shelter a friend, and I will not hide from him. But if harm should come to me because of him, whoever hears of it will beware of him.

Ecclesiasticus 22: 19 – 26 NRSV.

35

Be Careful of those you Trust

All counsellors praise the counsel they give, but some give counsel in their own interest. Be wary of a counsellor, and learn first what is his interest, for he will take thought for himself. He may cast the lot against you and tell you, your way is good, and then stand aside to see what happens to you.

Do not consult the one who regards you with suspicion; hide your intentions from those who are jealous of you. Do not consult with a woman about her rival or with a coward about war, with a merchant about business or with a buyer about selling, with a miser about generosity or with the merciless about kindness, with an idler about any work or with a seasonal labourer about completing his work, with a lazy servant about a big task — pay no attention to any advice they give.

But associate with a godly person whom you know to be a keeper of the commandments, who is like-minded with yourself, and who will grieve with you if you fail. And heed the counsel of your own heart, for no one is more faithful to you than it is.

For our own mind sometimes keeps us better informed than seven sentinels sitting high on a watchtower. But above all, pray to the Most High that he may direct your way in truth.

Ecclesiasticus 37: 7 – 15 NRSV.

God Loves You

Do you suppose that loving Parents would scold a child for falling down the stairs or go off and leave the child when it hurts? Not at all!
They would pick the child up, comfort and then encourage the child to keep on trying until the child learn to walk well.

Do you think that God will do any less for His child who is just beginning to walk? Impossible! Look to Him now in prayer and tell Him: *Thank you, Father, for holding my hand and teaching me how to walk. I am weak, but I know you will help me do the needful. Help me always to stand upright when I fall.*

You should know that God guides you in your Christian life through His Holy Spirit and His word. Pray always; it will help you eliminate doubts and walk without stumbling.

Be Prudent (1)

Do not winnow in every wind or follow every path. Stand firm for what you know, and let your speech be consistent. Be quick to hear but deliberate in answering. If you know what to say, answer your neighbour; if not, put your hand over your mouth.

Honour and dishonour come from speaking, and the tongue of mortals may be their downfall. Do not be called double-tongued, and do not lay traps with your tongue; for shame comes to the thief and severe condemnation to the double-tongued. In great and small matters, cause no harm, and do not become an enemy instead of a friend; for a bad name incurs shame and reproach; so, it is with the double-tongued sinner.

Do not fall into the grip of passion, or you may be torn apart as by a bull. Your leaves will be devoured, your fruit destroyed, and you will be left like a withered tree. Evil passion destroys those who have it and makes them the laughingstock of their enemies.

Ecclesiasticus 5: 9 – 15, 6: 1 – 4 NRSV.

Be Prudent (II)

Do not contend with the powerful, or you may fall into their hands. Do not quarrel with the rich, in case their resources outweigh yours; for gold has ruined many and has perverted the minds of kings. Do not argue with the loud of mouth, and do not heap wood on their fire.

Do not make fun of one who is ill-bred, or your ancestors may be insulted. Do not reproach one who is turning away from sin; remember that we all deserve punishment. Do not disdain one who is old, for some of us are also growing old. Do not rejoice over anyone's death; remember that we must all die. Do not slight the discourse of the sages, but busy yourself with their maxims; from them, you will learn discipline and how to serve princes. Do not ignore the discourse of the aged, for they themselves learned from their parents; from them, you learn how to understand and to give an answer when the need arises.

Do not kindle the coals of sinners, or you may be burned in their flaming fire. Do not let the insolent bring you to your feet, or they may lie in ambush against your words. Do not lend to someone stronger than you, but if you do lend anything, count it as a loss. Do not give surety beyond your means, but if you give surety, be prepared to pay.

Do not go to law against a judge, for the decision will favour him because of his standing. Do not go travelling with the reckless, or they will be burdensome to you; for they will act as they please, and through their folly, you will perish with them.

Do not pick a fight with the quick-tempered, and do not journey with them through a lonely country because bloodshed means nothing to them, and where no help is at hand, they will strike you down.

Do not consult with fools, for they cannot keep a secret. In the presence of strangers, do nothing that is to be kept secret, for you do not know what they will divulge. Do not reveal your thoughts to anyone, or you may ruin your happiness.

Ecclesiasticus 8: 1 – 19 NRSV.

Be Alert

Do not find fault before you investigate; examine first and then criticise. Do not answer before you listen or interrupt when another is speaking. Do not argue about a matter that does not concern you, and do not sit with sinners when they judge a case.

My child, do not busy yourself with many matters; if you multiply activities, you will not be held blameless. If you pursue, you will not overtake, and by fleeing, you will not escape. There are those who work and struggle and hurry but are so much more in want.

There are others who are slow and need help, who lack strength and abound in poverty, but the eyes of the Lord look kindly upon them; he lifts them out of their lowly condition and raises their heads to the amazement of the many.

Good things and bad, life and death, poverty and wealth, come from the Lord. The Lord's gift remains with the devout, and his favour brings lasting success. One becomes rich through diligence and self-denial, and the reward allotted to him is this: when he says, "I have found rest, and now I shall feast on my goods!" he does not know how long it will be until he leaves them to others and dies.

Stand by your agreement and attend to it and grow old in your work. Do not wonder at the works of a sinner, but trust in the Lord and keep at your job; for it is easy in the sight of the Lord to make the poor rich suddenly, in an instant. The blessing of the Lord is the reward of the pious, and quickly God causes his blessing to flourish. Do not say, "What do I need, and what further benefit can be mine?"

Do not say, "I have enough, and what harm can come to me now?" In the day of prosperity, adversity is forgotten, and in the day of adversity, prosperity is not remembered. For it is easy for the Lord on the day of death to reward individuals according to their conduct. An hour's misery makes one forget past delights, and at the close of one's life, one's deeds are revealed. Call no one happy before his death; by how he ends, a person becomes known.

Ecclesiasticus 11: 7 – 28 NRSV.

$$\boxed{40}$$

Be Positive

Nothing is more important than learning one's own value. We are children of God. We have a Divine purpose, and God has placed an immeasurable premium on us – just like we are.

God created man and woman to help Him develop this world and to rule over it.

He has opened the way for us to be successful, happy and productive.

Often the question is asked: Is it difficult?

In one sense, yes! Because we will have to adjust our thinking process, accept new ideas and learn to talk and act differently. And this can be TOUGH.

Once our lifestyle is fixed on a lower level, and we have decided who and what is to be blamed for our problems, it will be challenging for us to admit that our biggest enemy is ourselves – that our thoughts and words and deeds are the very problems, the failures and even many of the illnesses that have plagued us.

Suppose we view life from a fresh perspective and follow God's guidance. In that case, we can uncover a fulfilling way of living that encompasses physical, mental, material, and spiritual abundance. This new lifestyle promises a magnificent journey in God's abundant glory.

41

Be Wise in the Use of Wealth

Riches are inappropriate for a small-minded person, and of what use is wealth to a miser? What he denies himself he collects for others, and others will live in luxury on his goods. If one is mean to himself, to whom will he be generous? He will not enjoy his own riches.

Nothing is worse than one grudging to himself; this is the punishment for his meanness. If ever he does good, it is by mistake; and in the end, he reveals his meanness. A miser is an evil person; he turns away and disregards people. The eye of the greedy person is not satisfied with his share; greedy injustice withers the soul. A miser begrudges bread, and it lacks at his table.

According to your means, my child treats yourself well and present worthy offerings to the Lord. Remember that death does not tarry, and the decree of Hades has not been shown to you. Do good to friends before you die, and reach out and give to them as much as you can.

Do not deprive yourself of a day's enjoyment; do not let your share of desired good pass by you. Will you not leave the fruit of your labours to another, and what you acquired by toil to be divided by lot? Give, and take, and indulge yourself because, in Hades, one cannot look for luxury.

All living beings become old like a garment, for the decree from of old is, 'You must die!' Like abundant leaves on a spreading tree that sheds some and puts forth others, so are the generations of flesh and blood: one dies, and another is born. Every work decays and ceases to exist, and the one who made it will pass away with it.

Ecclesiasticus 13 – 14: 1 – 2 NRSV.

42

Ask Wisdom and Shun Foolishness (1)

Whoever keeps the law controls his thoughts, and the fulfilment of the fear of the Lord is wisdom. The one who is not clever cannot be taught, but there is a cleverness that increases bitterness. The knowledge of the wise will increase like a flood and their counsel like a life-giving spring. The mind of a fool is like a broken jar; it can hold no knowledge.

When an intelligent person hears a wise saying, he praises and adds to it; when a fool hears it, he laughs at it and throws it behind his back. A fool's chatter is like a burden on a journey, but delight is found in the speech of the intelligent. The utterance of a sensible person is sought in the assembly, and they ponder his words in their minds.

Like a house in ruins is wisdom to a fool, and to the ignorant, knowledge is talk that has no meaning. To a senseless person, education is a fetter on his feet, like manacles on his right hand. A fool raises his voice when he laughs, but the wise smile quietly. To the sensible person, education is like a golden ornament and a bracelet on the right arm.

The foot of a fool rushes into a house, but an experienced person waits respectfully outside. A boor peers into the house from the door, but a cultivated person remains outside. It is ill-mannered for a person to listen at the door; the discreet would be grieved by the disgrace.

The lips of babblers speak of what is not their concern, but the words of the prudent are weighed in the balance. The mind of fools is in their mouth, but the mouth of the wise is in their mind. When an ungodly person curses an adversary, he curses himself. A whisperer degrades himself and is hated in his neighbourhood.

Ecclesiasticus 21: 11 – 28 NRSV.

43

Ask Wisdom and Shun Foolishness (II)

The idler is like a filthy stone, and everyone hisses at his disgrace. The idler is like the filth of dunghills; anyone that picks it up will shake it off his hand.

It is a disgrace to be the father of an undisciplined son, and the birth of a daughter is a loss. A sensible daughter obtains a husband of her own, but one who acts shamefully is a grief to her father. An impudent daughter disgraces her father and husband and is despised by both. Like music in a time of mourning is an ill-timed conversation, but a thrashing and discipline are at all times wisdom.

Whoever teaches a fool is like one who glues potsherds together or rouses a sleeper from a deep slumber. Whoever tells a story to a fool tells it to a drowsy man, and at the end, he will say, "What is it?" Weep for the dead, for he has left the light behind; and weep for the fool, for he has left intelligence behind.

Weep less bitterly for the dead, for he is at rest, but the life of the fool is worse than death. Mourning for the dead lasts seven days, but it lasts all the days of their lives for the foolish or the ungodly. Do not talk much with a senseless person or visit an unintelligent person. Stay clear of him, or you may have trouble and be spattered when he shakes himself off. Avoid him, and you will find rest, and you will never be wearied by his lack of sense. What is heavier than lead? And what is its name except 'Fool'? Sand, salt, and a piece of iron are easier to bear than a stupid person.

A wooden beam firmly bonded into a building is not loosened by an earthquake, so the mind firmly resolved after due reflection will not be afraid in a crisis. A mind settled on an intelligent thought is like stucco decoration that makes a wall smooth. Fences set on a high place will not stand firm against the wind, so a timid mind with a fool's resolve will not stand firm against any fear.

Ecclesiasticus 22: 1 – 18 NRSV.

44

Avoid Disease

Like how a mother cares for her children's cleanliness and protects them from anything that could harm them, the Lord desires to safeguard our souls from anything that could make us spiritually ill.

Through His sacrifice on the cross at Calvary, He redeemed us, washed away our sins, and gifted us with a pure heart, which is essential for a sound spiritual existence.

Walking with the Lord daily and letting Him guide us is essential. We should avoid immoral behaviour and indecent pleasures, instead choosing to go where the Lord would go. Keeping our thoughts, words, and actions pure is essential.

Toxic attitudes and emotions such as anger, worry, envy, hatred, suspicion, fear, and impatience can harm our souls and body. They can cause digestive problems, ulcers, heart issues, and other illnesses. They choke out spiritual life and cause all kinds of trouble.

Certain spiritual vices can be detrimental to our well-being, such as pride, selfishness, unbelief, and stubbornness. These negative qualities can strip us of happiness and leave our souls feeling weak and unhealthy.

However, there is hope for those who feel spiritually unwell. Jesus is the Great Physician and can heal our spiritual, mental, and physical health. Approach Him with sincerity in prayer. He can provide the necessary support to help regain strength and vitality.

45

Avoid Evil

Do no evil, and evil will never overtake you. Stay away from wrong, and it will turn away from you. Do not sow in the furrows of injustice, and you will not reap a sevenfold crop.

Do not seek from the Lord high office or the seat of honour from the king. Do not assert your righteousness before the Lord or display your wisdom before the king. Do not seek to become a judge, or you may be unable to root out injustice; you may be partial to the powerful and so mar your integrity. Commit no offence against the public, and do not disgrace yourself among the people.

Do not commit a sin twice; not even for one will you go unpunished. Do not say, 'He will consider the great number of my gifts, and when I make an offering to the Most High God, he will accept it.' Do not grow weary when you pray; do not neglect to give alms. Do not ridicule a person who is embittered in spirit, for there is One who humbles and exalts. Do not devise a lie against your brother or do the same to a friend. Refuse to utter any lie, for it is a habit that results in no good. Do not babble in the assembly of the elders, and do not repeat yourself when you pray.

Do not hate hard labour or farm work, which was created by the Most High. Do not enrol in the ranks of sinners; remember that retribution does not delay. Humble yourself to the utmost, for the punishment of the ungodly is fire and worms.

Ecclesiasticus 7: 1 – 17 NRSV.

46

Learn from Wisdom

My child, from your youth, choose discipline, and when you have grey hair, you will still find wisdom. Come to her like one who prows and sows and wait for her good harvest. For when you cultivate her, you will toil but little, and soon you will eat of her produce. She seems very harsh to the undisciplined; fools cannot remain with her. She will be like a heavy stone to test them, and they will not delay in casting her aside. Wisdom is like her name; she is not readily perceived by many.

Listen, my child, and accept my judgment; do not reject my counsel. Put your feet into her fetters, and your neck into her collar. Bend your shoulders and carry her, and do not fret under her bonds. Come to her with all your soul and keep her ways with all your might. Search out and seek, and she will become known to you; and when you get hold of her, do not let her go. For, at last, you will find the rest she gives, and she will be changed into joy for you. Then her fetters will become for you a strong defence and her collar a glorious robe. Her yoke is a golden ornament, and her bonds a purple cord. You will wear her like a glorious robe and put her on like a splendid crown.

If you are willing, my child, you can be disciplined, and if you apply yourself, you will become clever. If you love to listen, you will gain knowledge; if you pay attention, you will become wise. Stand in the company of the elders. Who is wise? Attach yourself to such a one. Be ready to listen to every godly discourse, and let no wise proverbs escape you. If you see an intelligent person, rise early to visit him; let your foot wear out his doorstep. Reflect on the statutes of the Lord and meditate at all times on his commandments. It is he who will give insight to your mind, and your desire for wisdom will be granted.

Ecclesiasticus 6: 18 – 37 NRSV.

47

Being Modest

It is imperative that we exhibit modesty in our words, deeds, and physical appearance. Modesty is simply the opposite of pride and vanity. If we act as if we are superior to others and look down upon people who do things we would not do, we will drive them away from knowing the Lord instead of winning them for Him.

We must acknowledge that it is not within our rights to be proud of our identity, accomplishments, or possessions. We do not deserve a thing that God has done for us or given us. Remember that, without His mercy and work in our lives, we might be the most wretched, horrible sinners the world has ever known.

A self-centred and self-assured individual desires to be noticed by all. He may draw attention to himself with fashion trends, expensive clothing and jewellery, or by showing off his superior knowledge and abilities. He might attempt to draw attention to himself by deviating from accepted norms of attire and behaviour.

A proud person may boast of his spiritual experience and dedication to the Lord. A modest person will refrain from attempting to draw attention to themselves. He consciously tries to steer clear of fashion choices that are too outlandish, inappropriate, or offensive for those who follow the Lord's teachings.

48

Seize the moment, or it is Gone!

With the shortness of life comes the second reason to seek the Lord; thus, it is a great opportunity to seize every moment God has given us and make it count in our lives and those around us. Jesus once said, "The fields are white unto harvest," this implies countless possibilities and opportunities at our fingertips to do tremendous things for God. But harvest not gathered at the ripening is lost! This means that we would not always have those opportunities to work for God. We need to seize the moment and make it count for Him!

It is important to seek the Lord and make the most of the opportunities to serve Him that come our way. The little moments that add up to days and years should be dedicated to serving the Lord, as they can never be regained once lost. While we may come to Jesus and serve Him in our youth, the opportunities to serve Him richly may pass us by if we do not act on them. We cannot bring them back, renew them or relive them. Therefore, we must take hold of this moment before it slips away forever.

In life, there are moments when we are spiritually prepared! Indeed, there is a time when the Holy Spirit marshals all of the artillery of heaven to focus on the soul. Our heart is mellow, our minds malleable, our spirit open. At such an opportunity, God would use our voices to invite others to HIMSELF. Such opportunities appear infrequently, but it is always an opportunity to make a change. It is truly a privilege to be present and serve as the voice of God to someone's soul.

Those who do not seek the Lord are not sensitive to the spirit's voice. Caught in the confusion of the immediate, they lose both eye and ear for the eternal.

49

Building for Eternity

Whoever comes to me and does not hate father and mother, wife and children, brothers and sisters, yes and even life itself, cannot be my disciple.

Whoever does not carry the cross and follow me cannot be my disciple. Which of you intending to build a tower does not first sit down and estimate the cost to see whether he has enough to complete it?

Otherwise, when he has laid a foundation and cannot finish, all who see it will begin to ridicule him. Saying, This fellow began to build and was not able to finish.

Or what king, going to wage war against another king, will not sit down first and consider whether he is able with ten thousand to oppose the one who comes against him with twenty thousand? If he cannot, then, while the other is still far away, he sends a delegation and asks for the terms of peace.

Therefore, we cannot become the Lord's disciples if we do not give up earthly possessions.

Luke 14: 26 – 33 NRSV.

50

Think About Death

O death, how bitter is the thought of you to the one at peace among possessions, who has nothing to worry about, is prosperous in everything, and still is vigorous enough to enjoy food!

O death, how welcome is your sentence to one who is needy and failing in strength, worn down by age and anxious about everything, to one who is contrary and has lost all patience!

Do not fear death's decree for you; remember those who went before you and those who will come after. This is the Lord's decree for all flesh; why then should you reject the will of the Most High?

Whether life lasts ten years or a hundred or a thousand, there are no questions after death.

Ecclesiasticus 41: 1 – 4 NRSV.